I0893281

12 STORIES ABOUT HELPING IMMIGRANTS AND REFUGEES

by Samantha S. Bell

12 STORY LIBRARY
MORE TO EXPLORE

www.12StoryLibrary.com

Copyright © 2020 by 12-Story Library, Mankato, MN 56002. All rights reserved. No part of this book may be reproduced or utilized in any form or by any means without written permission from the publisher.

12-Story Library is an imprint of Bookstaves.

Photographs ©: Fibonacci Blue/CC2.0, cover, 1; Ververidis Vasilis/Shutterstock.com, 4; PD, 4; Mass Communication Specialist 2nd Class Kristopher Wilson/US Navy, 5; San José Public Library/CC2.0, 6; San José Public Library/CC2.0, 7; Wesley Bunnell/YouTube, 8; Jerry Dougherty/CC2.5, 9; Takver/CC2.0, 10; Jazzmany/Shutterstock.com, 11; PD, 11; Goran Jakus/Shutterstock.com, 12; Kanderson78/CC4.0, 12; Jazzmany/Shutterstock.com, 13; International Journalism Festival/CC2.0, 14; Vito Manzari/CC2.0, 15; Somerville Media Center/YouTube, 16; PD, 16; Matej Kastelic/Shutterstock.com, 17; E.Kryzhanivskyi/Shutterstock.com, 18; PD, 18; BalkansCat/Shutterstock.com, 19; Pirie MacDonald/Library of Congress, 20; UNHNY/YouTube, 20; UNHNY/YouTube, 21; Shawn Goldberg/Shutterstock.com, 21; United Nations/PD, 22; Djohan Shahrin/Shutterstock.com, 22; heb/CC3.0, 23; Aimee Brown/Oxfam East Africa/CC2.0, 24; PD, 24; Portland Press Herald/YouTube, 25; Green Card Voices/YouTube, 26; Education Futures/YouTube, 26; Green Card Voices/YouTube, 27; Rawpixel.com/Shutterstock.com, 28; Dmytro Zinkevych/Shutterstock.com, 29

ISBN
9781632357465 (hardcover)
9781632358554 (paperback)
9781645820314 (ebook)

Library of Congress Control Number: 2019938675

Printed in the United States of America
October 2019

About the Cover

A rally in Minneapolis, MN, in support of immigrants and refugees.

Access free, up-to-date content on this topic plus a full digital version of this book. Scan the QR code on page 31 or use your school's login at 12StoryLibrary.com.

Table of Contents

Doctors Without Borders: Healing Bodies and Minds 4

Denver Public Libraries: Bringing Immigrants Together 6

First Congregational Church of Old Lyme: Giving Sanctuary 8

Kaiserslautern: Offering Hope in Germany 10

Mercy Corps: Helping Refugees through Technology 12

Pietro Bartolo: Healing the Hopeless 14

The Welcome Project: Making Immigrants Feel at Home 16

Rooms for Refugees: Shelter in Hard Times 18

Riis Settlement: Helping Immigrants for Over a Century 20

UNICEF: Protecting the Children 22

Mid Coast New Mainers Group: Rebuilding Lives 24

Green Card Voices: Immigrants Telling Their Stories 26

Ways You Can Help 28

Glossary 30

Read More 31

Index 32

About the Author 32

1

Doctors Without Borders: Healing Bodies and Minds

A doctor checks a refugee to determine what medical care he might need.

Refugees are people who are forced to leave their home countries. Some leave to escape war, persecution, or hunger. Sometimes their towns are bombed. Or gangs take over their town or city. Some leave because their homes are destroyed by a storm or flood.

Doctors Without Borders is an organization made up of experienced doctors and nurses. They give refugees the medical care they need. They work with refugees in developing countries in the Middle East, Africa, and Latin America.

Wars and attacks in these areas have left millions of people homeless. Even if they find a safe place to stay, they still face many struggles. Sometimes they must crowd together in refugee camps. They may not get enough food to eat. There may be no clean water to drink. They are often sick and hungry. Doctors Without Borders tries to help.

70.8 million
Number of refugees worldwide in 2019

- Doctors Without Borders provides medical care to anyone who needs it.
- Sometimes they have to treat people and families who are on the move.
- The group wants to make people aware that others in the world are suffering.

Besides treating physical problems, the doctors and nurses also provide mental health care. Many refugees have experienced terrible things. They may be depressed, anxious, or frightened. The doctors try to help them recover.

Doctors Without Borders meets other needs as well. They take food to starving refugees. They provide refugees with hygiene kits. The kits help the people stay clean. Otherwise, deadly diseases will quickly spread.

Doctors evaulate a woman's injuries following the Haiti earthquake in 2010.

2 Denver Public Libraries: Bringing Immigrants Together

Immigrants attending a citizenship class.

15

Number of different languages spoken in the Denver Public Library's Plaza program

- Libraries in other US cities are creating similar programs.
- These include Los Angeles, California, Houston, Texas, and New York.
- They are using the Plaza program as a model.

Many immigrants move to Denver, Colorado. They come from many countries and speak more than 140 different languages or dialects. Settling into a new country and community is not easy. Denver's public library system has found a way to help.

In 2006, the library created the Plaza program. The program is offered at 10 of the library's branches. Through the program, immigrants can attend citizenship classes. They can learn English. They can do arts and crafts. Adults can find resources for legal matters and job searches. They can get child care. Students can get help with school. All the services are free of charge.

The Plaza program allows students to get help with school.

Around 1,800 immigrants and refugees use the services every month. When they come to the library, they find other people like them. They speak the same language. They are in the same situation. They have the same issues and face the same problems. They are able to help each other.

The Plaza program also helps build a feeling of community. Most of the participants return each week. They get to know each other. They get involved in neighborhood meetings. They become part of community activities.

WHAT'S IN A NAME?

The Plaza program was named after the plazas in Latin America. A plaza is a large public square. Government buildings are on the plaza. So is the largest church. There are places for people to sit and gather. The plaza is the center of the community.

3 First Congregational Church of Old Lyme: Giving Sanctuary

Sometimes immigrants don't have the legal documents required to stay in the United States. They may need more time to get them. In the meantime, they are at risk of being deported. Some of these immigrants seek help from churches. The churches offer them sanctuary, or safety. As long as the immigrants stay inside the church, authorities usually leave them alone. The immigrants don't have legal protection there. But most authorities won't go into a place of worship to arrest someone.

In 2000, Malik Naveed bin Rehman and his wife, Zahida Altaf, came to America from Pakistan. They hired lawyers to help them with their legal documents. The lawyers took their money but didn't help. In 2012, Rehman and Altaf had a daughter. Because she was born in the United States, she is an American citizen.

In 2017, the family was about to be deported. They found sanctuary in the First Congregational Church of

Rhemen and Altaf with their daughter at a press conference at the time they sought sanctuary in the First Congretional Church of Old Lyme.

Old Lyme, Connecticut. On March 19, 2018, they moved into the church. Their home was three Sunday school rooms in the basement. Their shower was a garden hose attached to a bathroom sink. They could go anywhere in the church. But the parents could not leave. They filled their time with activities like pottery-making and yoga.

The family found a new lawyer. On October 16, 2018, they ended their stay at the church and returned home. The church held a celebration for them.

The First Congregtional Church of Old Lyme.

7

Number of months the family lived in the church

- While at the church, Malik Naveed bin Rehman had to wear an ankle tracking bracelet.
- The bracelet told authorities where he was at all times.
- The bracelet was removed two days after Rehman left the church.

4

Kaiserslautern: Offering Hope in Germany

Kaiserslautern city residents make refugees feel welcome.

In 2015, Germany opened its borders to refugees. They came from Syria, Afghanistan, and Iraq. Many went to the small city of Kaiserslautern. City officials and residents worked hard to make the refugees feel welcome.

When refugees arrive in Kaiserslautern, they are given a place to stay. In some other cities and countries, refugees must live in tents or school gyms until housing is found for them. But in Kaiserslautern, the refugees live in small apartments.

There are many things to learn when coming to a new country. The refugees in Kaiserslautern learn how to speak German. They can take free classes. They also learn about German culture. The classes are often taught by volunteers.

Refugees receive money and medical care until they find jobs. Job centers

HEALING MINDS

Susan Sage is a psychologist with the Red Cross. She works with some of the refugees in Kaiserslautern's counseling center. Many experienced terrible things before coming to Germany. As a result, some are depressed or afraid. Some are very lonely. Some have nightmares about their experiences. Translators help Sage communicate with her patients. Sometimes she draws pictures to express what she wants to say.

80,000

Number of refugees who arrived in Germany from 2013 to 2018

- One in four of the war refugees are young men.
- Many had to leave their wives and girlfriends behind.
- The families hope to be reunited someday.

help them prepare for work. Volunteers and charities help them settle into their new life.

Refugee families arriving in the city live in small apartments until they settle into their new lives.

5

Mercy Corps: Helping Refugees through Technology

Cell phones are often the only way immigrants can communicate.

Based in Oregon, Mercy Corps is a worldwide organization. It brings together communities, corporations, and governments to help people in need, including refugees. Mercy Corps works with refugees in many countries. It provides them with money, food, and water. Mercy Corps also builds shelters and youth centers. It teaches important life skills refugees need to succeed in their new lives.

Many refugees have cell phones. Often this is their only way to communicate. Mercy Corps developed an app for refugees in Syria who were fleeing to Jordan. The app is called Khabrona.Info.

When refugees have to move quickly, they travel any way they can. Many times, they don't have information about where they are going. They don't know how long it will take to

40

Number of countries where Mercy Corps works

- The Mercy Corps app has a Facebook page, too.
- Refugees with internet access can join.
- Through the page, other refugees can answer their questions or offer comfort.

THINK ABOUT IT

You've just been asked to design an app for refugee students at your school. What will your app do? How will it help the students?

get there. The app helps them find information and resources they need. It helps them connect with family members.

Women refugees face extra risks. Often they don't have the same education as men. Some are widows and single mothers who must also support their families. Women are more likely to become crime victims. Khabrona.Info is especially helpful for them. It gives them access to reliable information. By using the app, they can contact Mercy Corps officers without risking their safety.

Mercy Corps builds shelters and youth centers so refugees can succeed in their new lives.

6

Pietro Bartolo: Healing the Hopeless

Pietro Bartolo is an Italian doctor. He runs the only clinic on a small island called Lampedusa. The island is in the middle of the Mediterranean Sea. Many refugees from Africa and the Middle East go to the island on their way to Europe.

The refugees arrive on the island by boat. Some are in terrible condition. Many have been tortured in their homelands. They have been shot, cut, or burned. Some refugees are injured as they travel. Most are dehydrated or have hypothermia. They are starving and exhausted.

Bartolo helps the refugees as they arrive. It is a difficult job. He sees how they have suffered. Many men, women, and children don't survive the trip. The boats they travel on

Pietro Bartolo in 2017.

Bartolo helps immigrants as they arrive on Lampedusa in crowed boats.

aren't safe. Dr. Bartolo sees these refugees, too. He wants other people to understand how much these people have suffered. He wants individuals and governments to step in and help them.

250,000+

Number of refugees Pietro Bartolo has met on Lampedusa

- The motto of Lampedusa is written on a mural on a pier.
- It says, "Protect people and not borders."
- Bartolo meets the refugees on that pier.

USING HIS EDUCATION FOR GOOD

Pietro Bartolo came from a large family of seven children. He was the only one who went to college. His father was a fisherman. The family could not afford to send anyone else. Bartolo studied medicine in Italy. He returned to Lampedusa after he graduated. He liked living by the sea. He also wanted to work for his people.

7

The Welcome Project: Making Immigrants Feel at Home

> The Youth Aspirations program helps young immigrants who are bilingual learn how to be interpreters.

The Welcome Project is based in Somerville, Massachusetts. Somerville is a multicultural community of people from many countries. The Welcome Project works with immigrants who live there.

The project has programs for immigrants of all ages. The programs help immigrants build leadership skills and take part in civic life. One example is the Youth Aspirations program. Young people who are bilingual learn how to be interpreters. Then they offer their services at community events and meetings. Some students from the program have gone on to college. Some have been hired as translators.

Other Welcome Project programs help immigrants adjust to living in a new country and culture. Adults who take English for Parents also learn about the school system and how it works. Then they can do a better job of advocating

The Welcome Project

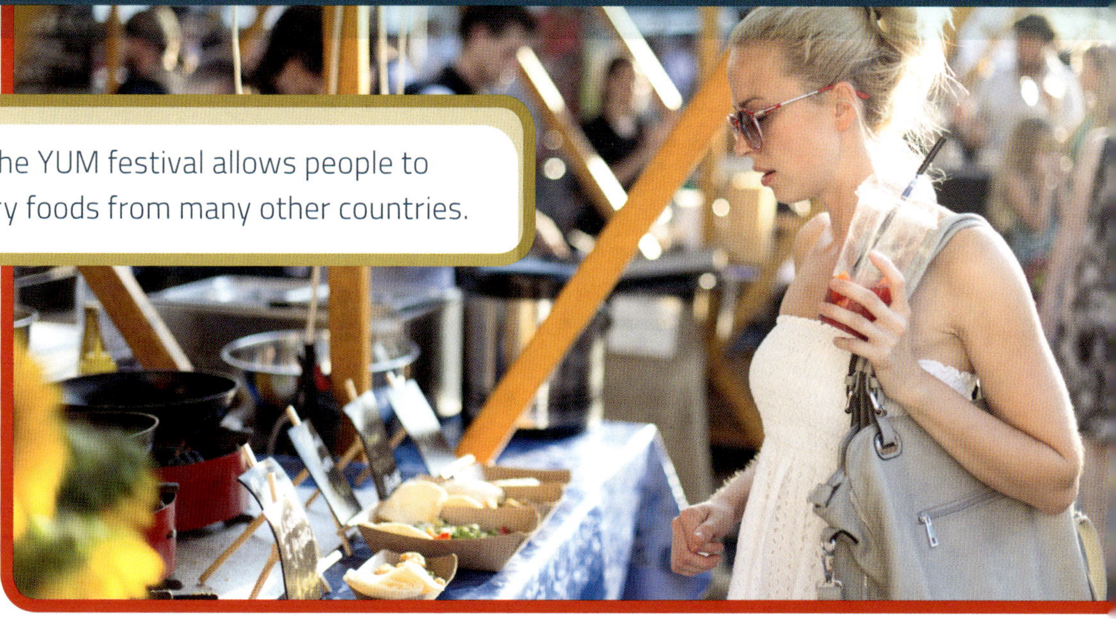

The YUM festival allows people to try foods from many other countries.

for their children. Adults can get help finding a job and applying for citizenship. They can even get parenting advice.

The Welcome Project helps immigrants find their roles in the Somerville community. They feel like part of the community, not like outsiders. The other residents of Somerville also benefit. They enjoy the unique diversity of their town.

1987

Year when the Welcome Project was founded

- Immigrants began coming to Somerville in the 1980s. They came from Vietnam, Haiti, and Central America.
- Some of the immigrants were harassed and threatened by people in the community.
- Doctors, nurses, pastors, city officials, and families created the Welcome Project to bring the community together.

A TASTY CELEBRATION

Each year, Somerville hosts the YUM festival. Foods made by immigrants from different countries is available. People can buy tickets to try the different food. Restaurants donate the food, so all the money goes to the Welcome Project.

8

Rooms for Refugees: Shelter in Hard Times

Refugee children without their parents are welcomed into loving homes.

POSITIVE ACTION
WORKING TOGETHER TO REBUILD LIVES

Positive Action in Housing (PAIH) is a charity based in Glasgow, Scotland. In 2002, it started a program called Room for Refugees in Scotland and the United Kingdom. The program connects refugees and people with spare rooms who are willing to let refugees stay there for a while. Sometimes refugee children arrive without their parents. They are placed in homes with loving families.

Many of the refugees come from Syria. Others come from Iraq, Iran, or Afghanistan. The refugees may need a place to stay for a week. Some need housing for a month. Some stay with their hosts for years.

Caseworkers try to help refugees clear up their legal and housing situations. Having a place to stay helps. Refugees without shelter may be taken to detention centers. Other refugees at risk include those who are sick, older refugees, and families.

Anyone can offer a room to a refugee. Hosts come from all different backgrounds. Most of the refugees live in Glasgow. Some live in Edinburgh, another city in Scotland. Some live in London, England. Hosts and refugees can live anywhere. When refugees have places to stay, they can think about other important things. They can focus on education, look for work, and start rebuilding their lives.

7,500

Number of Room for Refugees hosts in 2018

- Room for Refuges began with 50 hosts.
- In 2015, people all over the world heard about a three-year-old Syrian boy named Alan Kurdi. He drowned when his family tried to reach a Greek island.
- After that, many more people wanted to help.

Hosts welcome refugees into their homes so they can start rebuilding their lives.

9 Riis Settlement: Helping Immigrants for Over a Century

In 1888, a group of church women in New York wanted to do something for the poor immigrants who were coming into the city. They asked a Danish American man named Jacob A. Riis for help. Riis was a photojournalist and a social activist. Together they started a new settlement house. This is a place where community members can come for programs, services, and activities. In 1901, it was renamed the Jacob A. Riis Neighborhood Settlement House.

Jacob A. Riis in 1905.

Riis Settlement
"a place to grow"

Over 100 years later, the Riis Settlement is still helping immigrants in Long Island City and Queens, New York. Programs today include English language classes and after-school activities. They also include services for seniors.

Many immigrants want to become US citizens. But the process is

The Riis Settlement in New York.

complicated and can be confusing. In 2009, the Riis Settlement started a new legal services program. Now immigrants can receive free legal advice. Lawyers help them figure out their issues. They help them find a path to citizenship.

IN THEIR SHOES

When Jacob Riis first came to America in 1870, he was very poor. He had to take any job he could find. He saw firsthand the crime, sickness, and hunger in areas where poor immigrants lived. Eventually he got a job as a police reporter. He wrote about what he saw. He taught himself photography so he could take pictures, too. That way, he could show the world.

450

Number of immigrants the Riis Settlement aims to help each year

- Jacob Riis was one of the first people in America to use flash photography.
- This meant he could take pictures of the dark, overcrowded buildings and basements where poor people lived.
- He published his photos in a book to make people aware of the problem.

10

UNICEF: Protecting the Children

During World War II (1939–1945), much of Europe was under attack. By the time the war ended, many parts of Europe had been badly damaged or destroyed. The people needed food and medicine. In 1946, UNICEF was created to help children in Europe, China, and the Middle East. The next year, UNICEF in the United States began.

UNICEF is the United Nations Children's Fund. The organization works to save and protect the world's most vulnerable children. It helps provide many things children need to survive and have a brighter future.

Many of the children UNICEF helps are refugees. Some live in large refugee camps. UNICEF supplies things like water and tents. It sponsors health care centers where children can get free medical care and immunizations. UNICEF also provides education for children and services for teens.

UNICEF helps refugee children who are traveling. Sometimes the children travel with their families. But many times, they are traveling alone. With no one to protect them, they may

Children in Bangladesh with backpacks filled with supplies from UNICEF.

A UNICEF School-in-a-Box contains basic supplies for one teacher and 40 students.

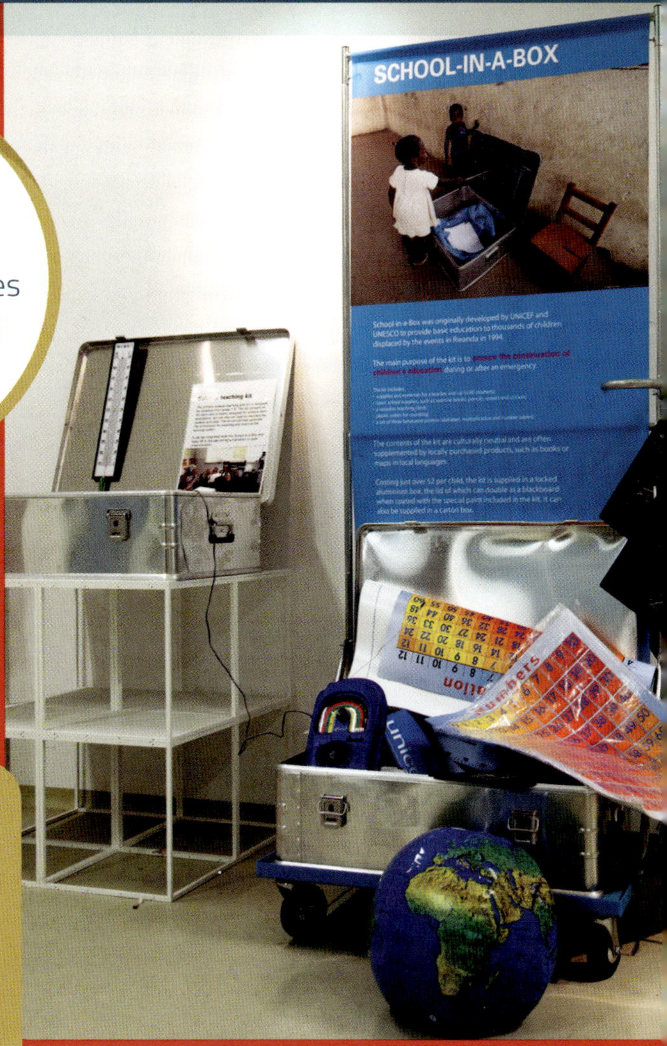

suffer violence or abuse. The children need someone to take care of them. UNICEF tries to keep them safe.

190

Number of countries and territories where UNICEF is working

- UNICEF stands for United Nations International Children's Emergency Fund. In 1953, that was shortened to United Nations Children's Fund.
- UNICEF was started by the United Nations General Assembly.
- Since 1947, people have given over $7.7 billion in donations to support UNICEF's mission.

THINK ABOUT IT

Many refugee children are separated from their parents. What are some things they might worry about? How do you think they feel when UNICEF workers help them?

11 Mid Coast New Mainers Group: Rebuilding Lives

Immigrants who move to Maine are called New Mainers. Most settle in larger cities like Portland. But some want to move to smaller towns.

These immigrants must be more self-reliant, since smaller towns don't offer as many public services as cities.

7

Number of churches represented in the Mid Coast New Mainers Group

- The group makes the community aware that the immigrants are there.
- Group members contact the library and schools.
- They contact the police and city groups so they can help the immigrants, too.

Mid Coast New Mainers Group

In 2016, members of the Universal Unitarian Church at Brunswick, Maine, wanted to do something to help. They held a community meeting. Members of churches in

The support group hosts dinners for immigrants so they can become familiar with their community.

THINK ABOUT IT

Imagine that a new student has just joined your class at school. The student is an immigrant. What can you do to make the student feel welcome?

Bath and Topsham came. Together they formed the Mid Coast New Mainers Group.

The group began by collecting furniture for new immigrant families. They hosted a multicultural dinner. In December 2017, they helped their first family settle in Bath. A mother and her two children had come from West Africa. The group helped the mother get an apartment and find a job. They helped her enroll in classes to become a nurse. They helped the children get started in school. They paid for activities such as swimming lessons and camps. Volunteer drivers took the family where they needed to go.

When other New Mainers arrive, the people in the community support them in many ways. Some give to meet a need, such as a bed or used car. Others help immigrants fill out job applications. They provide car rides or day care. Every family is assigned a mentor. The mentor helps the family manage day-to-day activities in a new culture.

12

Green Card Voices: Immigrants Telling Their Stories

There are many stereotypes about immigrants. One is that most immigrants are in the country illegally. Another is that immigrants don't have many skills. Some people think immigrants commit a lot of crimes.

Tea Rozman Clark in 2017.

But an immigrant named Tea Rozman Clark is working to break stereotypes. In 2013, Clark helped start Green Card Voices (GCV). The organization collects first-person stories told by individual immigrants. It shares the stories in books and videos, online and in traveling exhibits. Each story is a glimpse into a person's life.

GCV has recorded stories by immigrants in Minnesota, New York, New Jersey, and California. These include a dancer from Ecuador, a former MLB player from Cuba, and a journalist from Somalia. GCV also publishes books of stories by immigrant students. Many of the students have gone through hard times. But they are working toward

a brighter future. Another book tells the stories of immigrant and refugee business owners.

Schools, communities, and people anywhere can learn about the real lives of real immigrants. This builds empathy and understanding. GCV is replacing stereotypes with stories.

400
Approximate number of immigrants Tea Rozman Clark has interviewed

- The immigrants came from over 120 countries.
- Green Card Voices began in Minneapolis, Minnesota.
- More than 10,000 GCV books have been sold.

ON A MISSION

Tea Rozman Clark was born in Yugoslavia. When she was 15 years old, war broke out in her country. She worked in the refugee camps. She decided then that she would keep helping refugees. Clark came to the United States to attend college and graduate school. During her studies, she realized how important it is for people to tell their stories.

Ways You Can Help

- Welcome immigrants and refugees to your school, your neighborhood, and your place of worship.
- Help classmates from other countries with their homework.
- Learn about the food and customs of others.
- Find out about the refugee services in your town or city. Ask what you can do to help.

- Raise money for refugees with fundraisers like bake sales and yard sales.
- Learn if there's a place nearby that collects household goods for refugees and immigrants. Get together with your friends and gather items to donate.
- Help with a furniture drive for new families.
- Invite a new student to sit with you during lunch.
- Help a classmate learn English.
- Collect school supplies for new students from other countries.

Glossary

activist
A person who believes in forceful action to make a change.

advocate
To support or speak out about a cause, person, or group.

bilingual
Able to speak two languages.

charity
An organization that gives aid to people in need.

deport
To force a person who is not a citizen to leave a country.

detention center
A place where people are held for a period of time while waiting for legal action.

developing country
A poor country that is trying to become more advanced.

dialect
A variation of a language used by members of a certain group or class.

diversity
Differences among the people in a community.

hygiene
Cleanliness activities that support good health.

hypothermia
A condition when a person's body temperature is dangerously low.

immunization
A treatment with a vaccine that helps prevent disease.

persecution
When people are treated unfairly because of their race or beliefs.

photojournalist
A journalist who communicates the news through photographs.

self-reliant
Able to do things without needing help from others.

stereotype
An idea that many people have about a group of people that may be untrue or only partly true.

Read More

Creager, Ellen. *Life as a Syrian American.* New York: PowerKids Press, 2018.

Henzel, Cynthia. *Mexican Immigrants: In Their Shoes.* Mankato, MN: Childs World, 2017.

Roberts, Ceri. *Refugees and Migrants.* Hauppauge, NY: B.E.S. Publishing, 2017.

Visit 12StoryLibrary.com

Scan the code or use your school's login at **12StoryLibrary.com** for recent updates about this topic and a full digital version of this book. Enjoy free access to:

- **Digital ebook**
- **Breaking news updates**
- **Live content feeds**
- **Videos, interactive maps, and graphics**
- **Additional web resources**

Note to educators: Visit 12StoryLibrary.com/register to sign up for free premium website access. Enjoy live content plus a full digital version of every 12-Story Library book you own for every student at your school.

Index

Bartolo, Pietro, 14-15

church sanctuary, 8-9
community programs, 7, 16-17, 20, 24-25

Doctors Without Borders, 4-5

finding jobs, 11

Green Card Voices (GCV), 26-27

housing, 10, 20

immigrant stories, 26-27

legal services, 6, 18, 21

medical care, 4-5, 11, 14, 22
mental care, 4-5, 11
Mercy Corps, 12-13
Mid Coast New Mainers Group, 24-25

Plaza program, 6-7
Positive Action in Housing (PAIH), 18-19
protecting children, 22-23

resources, 6-7, 13
Riis, Jacob A., 20-21
Rooms for Refugees, 18-19

settlement house, 20-21
shelters, 12, 18

United Nations Children's Fund (UNICEF), 22-23

ways to help, 28-29
Welcome Project, 16-17

About the Author

Samantha S. Bell lives in upstate South Carolina with her family and lots of animals. She is the author of more than 100 nonfiction books for children.

READ MORE FROM 12-STORY LIBRARY

Every 12-Story Library Book is available in many fomats. For more information, visit **12StoryLibrary.com**